the song of songs

the SONG of SONGS

which is solomon's

illustrated by katie thamer

introduction by
reverend steven mc claskey

a star and elephant book
the green tiger press
1981

The Song of Songs - King James Version
Illustrations copyright © 1981 by Katie Thamer
Introduction copyright © 1981 by Reverend Steven McClaskey

The Green Tiger Press
La Jolla, California 92038

ISBN 0-914676-46-6
First Edition
First Printing

INTRODUCTION

The Song of Songs is somewhat of an oddity, an unusual book which begins, "Let him kiss me with the kisses of his mouth," and runs headlong in a glorious riot of passion, pining, and catch-as-catch-can embraces. There is the beloved leaping upon the mountains, and the cedary bower where love's cup is filled to the brim. There is an anxious night watch for the lover, and wanderings through city streets when he cannot be found. There is the mysterious group of shadowy attendants who, following the lovers, long to share vicariously in their delights. There are lavish descriptions of the body and of the sweets, fragrances, and flowers of amorous play. You may enjoy its deliciousness and peculiarity, but soon you will notice that it appears to go nowhere. It seems a mere snippet from some now faceless lover's diary, detailing the passion and pleasure, the exultation and despair, of one brief, shining moment in the lives of a man and a woman.

There are, however, things in our experience which are not what they seem, and the Song of Songs is one of them. It is a love song, a poem of desire and consummation, but of a very uncommon sort. Its joys are not simply those of the lovers figured in its verse — they are invitations, promises of rewards that may be ours. To discover them, however, we must make a roundabout approach. I propose to present some signposts which will not describe the destination so much as points of interest along the way. If followed, they will lead up to the front gate into the garden of the Song. They will, in addition, provide some commentary on the landscape.

THE CROSSROADS OF BELIEF

It may be disconcerting, at first, to discover that the Song of Songs is a book of the Bible. After all, what has the love-making of a King and a Shulamite to do with the things of God? Scripture's province is those things which are set apart from all that is unconsecrated. If we are looking for disclosures or revelations of God, we are disinclined to wander into strange bedrooms to find them. The Song can be embarrassing, for it seems more likely to arouse lasciviousness than the sacred devotion of scripture.

Because of its sensuousness, the status of the Song of Songs was already a long-disputed question when the canon of scripture came to be established. The Song now has an established place in the Hebrew Scriptures or, for Christians, the Old Testament. But in the Mishnah, the authoritative collection of Jewish Oral Law, we find considerable disagreement regarding the sacred value of the Song.

The major controversy surrounding the book lies in its erotic content, but the obscurity of its origins also contributes to its questionable status. By the time of the Synod of Jamnia, around 100 A.D., which determined the extent of the Hebrew bible, the Song was at least a thousand years old. Though its authorship was traditionally ascribed to Solomon, many considered its theme too base for Israel's sage king. Were Solomon's intentions less than pious? Long before Jamnia the Song was bandied about as a bawdy-house wine song. Could not Solomon have intended it to be just such an entertainment?

Not once is God mentioned in the Song. There are no revelations to which we would prefix, "Thus saith the Lord." The absence of any internal evidence for the sacred character of the book has produced a number of imaginative interpretations, especially in the last two centuries. The Song has been variously described as a secular love ballad, the remnants of a lost fertility cult liturgy, a dream, a two- or perhaps three-character drama with a chorus, and a cycle of wedding songs belonging to ancient nuptial festivities. There are other more esoteric interpretations, but all suffer from the same limitation — there is no evidence which makes any single explanation irrefutable.

Let us consider the most obvious interpretation — the Song as a secular love ballad. When it is compared to other contemporaneous Eastern love songs, a glaring discrepancy appears. In not one of the secular love songs is the lover's suit pressed by the female. In the cultures of the time, the Shulamite's boldness would have been appalling. Calling the song a secular love ballad would, then, suggest that it was written by some old-world feminist — unlikely considering the patriarachal nature of early Hebrew society.

Ultimately, each of us must choose what to believe about the Song of Songs. We find ourselves in that common position where belief is not supported by the evidence, but evidence is interpreted by belief. If I do not believe in ghosts, I shall dismiss the misty shape in the graveyard as incandescent swamp gas, an abberation of my impressionable imagination, or the trick of pranksters. Just this far we are free: nothing can compel our belief. How we interpret the Song is the result of what we believe it to be, and not the other way around.

TAKE OFF YOUR SHOES, YOU ARE ON HOLY GROUND

However, our beliefs must bow at the bar of truth. They are justified or falsified by reality. Often our knowledge of things depends not on our own experience but on the authority of another. Our knowledge of history, technology, the arts, even of our own bodies and souls is usually acquired this way. True, at the root of each of us is some certainty validated only by our own experience, but much more is known by faith.

The best authorities, however, will tell us that with the advantage of a wider experience we can test the truth of their assertions. The authorities who placed the Song of Songs among the sacred writing did so in the confidence that their judgment was open to confirmation by anyone who would put the Song to the test. Indeed, it was their own use of the book that convinced them of its merit. Andrew Harper writes in his commentary on the Song of Songs, in the *Cambridge Bible:*

> When therefore, we find, as we certainly do find, that the Song of Solomon was probably received into the Canon mainly in the sense which made it a text-book of the love of God to the church or the individual soul, and of its reciprocal love to God: if we find that it has from earliest times edified the Church by inspiring some of its finest minds and many of its most saintly lovers of God to the fullest expression of their highest thoughts, if we find that more than any other book of scripture it has kept men in mind of the fact that their highest moments, the moments when earthly love has lost all its carnality and all its selfishness, and has become a pure flame of utter devotion, are typical of what the relation between the soul and God ought to be, then it does seem unduly bold to deny that the author may have intended the more recondite spiritual reference.

The sacred interpretation of the Song of Songs as a kind of divine guidebook is an invitation to use it in a special way. As a holy hymn it is, mysteriously, a vehicle of transport. Considered any other way, it is an eccentric antique, more at home in the curiousity shop than in the Bible.

THE GARDEN OF THE MUSE POLYHYMNIA

The Song of Songs, like the Psalms, is essentially a ritual of devotion: a means, through discipline, to raise the mind, heart and will in love to God. We moderns are uncomfortable with ritual. We believe spontaneity to be more expressive of true, untrammeled human nature. The special value of ritual has been lucidly expressed by C.S. Lewis in *A Preface to Paradise Lost:*

> It is a pattern imposed on the mere flux of our feelings by reason and will, which renders pleasures less fugitive and griefs more endurable, which hand over to power of wise custom the task (to which the individual and his moods are so inadequate) of being festive or sober, gay or reverent, when we choose to be, and not at the bidding of chance.

The task of loving God, which scripture sets before us as our destiny and enduring happiness, does not come spontaneously or easily. Like the athlete who sets his or her heart on the prize, we must be shaped by rigorous training. Through ritual we can apply ourselves to the task of loving God by choice, and not leave the achievement to our inconstant whim. The Song of Songs, then, is a spiritual exercise to be taken up again and again in practice toward perfect love.

The capacity of the Song's ritual movement to shape our inner life proceeds from its poetry. The oriental flavor and imagery are foreign to us, but repeated use of the poem will amend that. The Song of Songs should be read aloud. It is, after all, a hymn, a musical utterance. There is a primordial power in the spoken word, of which silent reading is but a shadow. When we read aloud, more of our faculties aid in holding our attention, so a poem read aloud can move and engulf us in a way that words over which we merely run our eyes cannot.

The pattern of ritual in the Song is not mechanical. It defies translation into a neat list of spiritual rules. One cannot extract a formula of devotion from the poetry, for the poetry is itself the formula.

Milton said that true poetry is "simple, sensuous, and passionate," which describes exactly the Song's character. The reasons the Song works as a discipline, and the way it works, are bound up with the kind of utterance it is. The poetry is integral, not expendable, the warp and woof of the method itself.

In a poem of devotional love we will not find meaning as we would expect to find it in an essay on "How to Pray." Instead we find love itself. This explains much of the puzzlement surrounding the Song. Poetry creates its own language and there is more music in it than grammar. Ordinary words are used, but elusively, in a way that does not so much signify as tingle and resonate. In poetry words go outside themselves; they become a mystic wind playing on the aeolian harp of the human heart; they body forth the form of things unknown. They are words we know and yet do not know, a subtly alien arrangement of familiar things. Through poetry we are made to feel what the poet feels. A door is opened and we are ushered into a world we have never known. The Song of Songs is a vibration of experience, the progressive spiritual movement toward God in love.

The Song sets up a resonance of emotion in the reader, in order to reach us on a level even deeper than feeling. St. Bernard of Clairvaux, one of the great Christian commentators on the Song, has said that the Song "is not a cry from the mouth, but the gladness of the heart, not the sounding of the lips, but the impulse and emotion of joys within; not a concert of words, but of wills moving in harmony." The Song's purpose is to stir what is at the very root of our being. It does not so much elevate our impulses as send them down to the wellspring of desire. Emotional love, the beginning of love for every individual, remains but a shadow until the will moves in unison with it toward the beloved. If the will fails to move, love becomes a fleeting shadow. Mature love is rooted not in the chance of emotions but in the repeated act of choosing. It is essentially the movement toward harmony of the human will with the divine will.

Will, the deepest desire in us, is not characterized by felt sensations. It is that aspect of our human nature which most closely resembles God, for its nature is simply to act.

The will is the seat of order for our lives; its business is the establishment of priorities, freeing the individual from the irrationality of desire. It enables us to rise above the chaos of feelings and live by choice. This power of the will is an achievement won with great difficulty. The will itself needs training, and like Plato's sage kings, it can be disciplined by the very subjects it is to rule. Feelings, shaped into ritual, can train the will into a firm habit of choice. By repeated and deliberate movement of the will toward the object of desire, a pattern can be established which, in the end, will free us from the tyranny of undisciplined emotions. This is, no doubt, one purpose of that enthusiasm which new converts feel for God. Having once turned toward Him, the emotions then marshal to make the movement habitual.

The Song would also rally our emotions, on a more profound level, to the same service. It takes over when our natural enthusiasm wanes (as it always does). Its purpose is not merely to evoke in us the delights of divine scripture and the pleasure of experience, but to discipline the will into a habitual movement toward God which will continue when both the Song and our initial feelings have ended.

The Song cannot coerce the will into a love for God, any more than a great musical score can make someone a pianist. But once one wishes to become a musician, once the will is there, the score can be an invaluable help toward mastery. So it is with the Song of Songs. It is a poem that will transform novices into masters of love.

THE FOUNTAIN OF PRAYER

The Song of Songs, then, is a ritual of devotion. Like all ritual, it is an empty ceremony, a form requiring content. It cannot create devotion any more than a musical score can create music without an instrument. The instrument for singing the Song of Songs is prayer. Only when the Song is prayed does it become perfectly what it is — music made between divine and human lovers. If I take up the Song without the intention of prayer, it will remain an empty and, finally, dissatisfying form.

We do not find praying an easy occupation, and so we shrink from it. To juggle an aphorism of G. K. Chesterton, prayer has not been tried and found wanting; it is, too often, found difficult and left untried. It is, however, easier to live by prayer than to live without it. If we wish to carry the lighter burden, the Song can be of invaluable assistance. But we must bring to it the intention of looking to God. Prayer, nurtured, moved, and carried along by the passion of the Song, becomes a prayer of love, a transport of delight.

> Devotion borrows Music's tone,
> And Music took Devotion's wing
> And like the bird that hails the sun,
> They soar to heaven, and soaring sing.
> (The Hermit of St. Clement's Well)

THE DOORWAY TO DISCOVERY

The Song of Songs is a mystical prayer. Unfortunately, to so name it makes it for many moderns either infinitely remote, or the object of a voguish, occult fascination. Mysticism, properly understood, implies neither of these things. It is meant to be a tool for every day use.

Since the fall of man, Scripture tells us, everyone begins life with a crippling disadvantage. While revelation and conscience may teach us what is true and good, and what God demands of us, we are not equal to the task. The justice, mercy, and humility which we know, we are unable to accomplish. We are clothed in weakness.

If we do not always have the power to act, we do always have the power to pray, which wins for us the power to act. Approaching God in prayer makes it possible for us to approach Him in character, to undergo that self-change which transforms impotence and death into strength and life. This is the mystical way — pray, then act. It is the means by which one can become God-like, "a partaker of the divine nature." (II Peter 1:4) And so our deepest desire is satisfied.

The Song of Songs is an aid to this mystical way. It does not tell us about God or what He is doing for us. It is, rather, an introduction to Him. It is not a representation of the Word; it is a door through which we meet him for ourselves. It does not tell us how to live, but places at our disposal a pattern of interior movement, the straight and narrow way of life itself.

TEMPLE OF LOVE

The Song of Songs is a song of love. But what are we to make of its unmistakably sensuous and erotic character? Interestingly, the traditional interpretations of the Song skirt the question by treating the love-making as allegory, the story of the love between God and the human soul veiled in the figure of sexuality. The erotic imagery of the poem is cast as explanatory symbols of spiritual intercourse. Take for example, this coquettish passage:

> My beloved is like a roe or a young hart:
> behold, he standeth behind our wall,
> He looketh forth at the window,
> Shewing himself through the lattice.

St. Bernard interprets the wall as the flesh that hides our Lord from us, and the apertures are those human senses through which we gain experience, though imperfectly perceived, of Him. This is a helpful interpretation and certainly worth pondering. But the student soon discovers that the allegorical interpretation leads not so much to an explanation of the poem, as to the development of a new prose mystery in which the soul and God replace the bride and bridegroom, and exchanges of love cease to be passionate and become reflective. Light takes the place of warmth. But this interpretation is only superficially more lucid than the Song taken at face value. In the long run it can be quite as baffling and much less interesting.

The orthodox interpretations of the song instruct initiates, but the Song itself makes initiates. It is the fire of desire and not love's light that is its mainspring. Passion rather than knowledge is the source of its power.

The controversy over the eroticism in the Song remains, in spite of the fundamental truth that we can approach God through sensible things, using them as a ladder by which we may ascend to Him, or as a mirror in which we may find Him. Creation not only bears the stamp of the creator, revealing the hand behind the handiwork, but it mysteriously bears the Creator Himself. He is not far off but nigh. Beginning with what we know, we can approach what we do not know.

This is especially true of the love between a man and a woman. The biblical view is that all love is centered in God. Love is expressed, in part, by sexuality, created by God to be the physical reflection of the fecund glory of divine life. A man and a woman becomes one flesh, and in this union life is conceived. The Bible uses human love to communicate the love of God, not only because it is the best metaphor at hand, but because human love is derived from the divine. Physical love is the expression of divine love appropriate to embodied creatures. It is not a human way of speaking about God, but a divine way of speaking about man. Finally, it is not we who explain God, but He who explains us.

For this reason, sexual love is holy, and religion has hedged it about with the moral law, enshrining it within the sacrament of holy matrimony. However, the bulwark that girds sex is not for its preservation but ours. We are no threat to it, but if we misuse it we place ourselves in grave danger. Sexuality is the flame of passion, and, as with all fire, if we do not respect its nature we shall reap the consequences.

Lust, adultery and fornication are not corruptions of physical love, but of the people who embrace them. They are not abuses of sexuality, but of the soul. As with all things holy, sex cannot be defiled, for God is the warden, the guardian, of all that is holy. Derived from God's love, sexual love confers the benefits of its origin on those who share its secrets. In the nuptial bed, it is not sexuality which is consecrated but a man and a woman.

Sexual sin consists in desiring the pleasure of union while denying its divinely intended effect. That does not mean that denial prevents the effect. No flame kindled by God can be snuffed by the breath of man. If, however, we will not be transformed by that fire, we will be consumed by it. Intercourse between a man and woman creates union. It is either a saving or an avenging union.

From the biblical perspective, the desire of husband and wife for each other, consummated in sexual union, becomes the inspiration for the holy music of the Song of Songs. The Song itself, like sex, can be a tool of sanctification. We have already considered the poetic means by which the Song resonates desire. In marriage, desire works towards the union of love through the sexual act itself. In the Song, desire moves straight from the human heart to the divine heart — its own birthplace. The Song becomes a mystical body of love bearing our heart, mind, and soul into the arms of our divine lover. From a love known we move to a love unknown.

Like St. Mary we may be inclined to ask, "How shall this be?" Desire, after all, is physical, and its satisfaction consists of sexual expression. Can passion bear such a heavy burden as the love of God? Can pure spirit be loved passionately?

Let desire speak for itself, as it does on the lips of lovers and poets. There we hear the language of eternity and splendor. In the physical, lovers find a rapture so great that it burst the confines of ordinary experience.

> Who conceives, what bards devise
> that heaven is placed in Celia's eyes?

In pointing out that an ordinary girl becomes a goddess in her lover's eyes, Matthew Prior, in the above lines, states a truism that needs no justification. Desire gives lovers their vision. Desire discerns in the body something more than flesh.

> From the graced decorum of the hair,
> Ev'n to the tingling sweet
> Soles of the simply earth-confiding feet
> And from the inmost heart
> Outward unto the thin
> Silk curtains of the skin
> Every least part
> Astonish'd hears
> And sweet replies to some like region of the spheres.

Thus writes Coventry Patmore, and, not only for him but for every lover, the body is 'compact of heavenly qualities,' for only heaven is broad enough to encompass the scope of desire. In human passion there is more than the yearning of body for body; there is admiration and wonder, a sweet and breathless awe, a longing to worship. The true end of desire is this holy rapture: to be ravished by heaven in the flesh. All longing is finally a spiritual longing for holy union with God.

The Scriptures present the body as a temple, that holy place where the Spirit of God dwells on earth. It is bigger inside than out — capable of containing the deep heaven of God in humanity. Using the temple rite and mysteries, the Song of Songs brings us toward worship, adoration, and redemption. But the wise custom of the best of songs is a discipline of delight, an instruction by ecstacy, through a passion and miracle of words.

Reverend Steven McClaskey

BRIDE LET him kiss me with
the kisses of his mouth:
for thy love is better than wine ·
because of the savour of thy good
ointments thy name is as ointment
poured forth,
therefore do the virgins love thee ·
draw me, we will run after thee :
the king hath brought me into his
chambers :

CHORUS we will be glad and rejoice in thee,
we will remember thy love more than
wine : the upright love thee ·

BRIDE I am black, but comely, o ye daughters
of jerusalem, as the tents of kedar,
as the curtains of solomon ·
Look not upon me, because I am black,
because the sun hath looked upon me:
my mother's children were angry
with me; they made me the keeper
of the vineyards;
but mine own vineyard have I not kept ·
tell me, o thou whom my soul loveth,

where thou feedest, where thou makest thy flock to rest at noon: for why should I be as one that turneth aside by the flocks of thy companions?

BRIDEGROOM If thou know not, o thou fairest among women, go thy way forth by the footsteps of the flock, and feed thy kids beside the shepherds' tents.
I have compared thee, o my love, to a company of horses in pharaoh's chariots.
Thy cheeks are comely with rows of jewels, thy neck with chains of gold.

CHORUS We will make thee borders of gold with studs of silver.

BRIDE While the king sitteth at his table, my spikenard sendeth forth the smell thereof.
A bundle of myrrh is my well beloved unto me; he shall lie all night betwixt my breasts.
My beloved is unto me as a cluster of camphire in the vineyards of en-gedi.

BRIDEGROOM Behold, thou art fair, my love;

BEHOLD, THOU ART FAIR, MY LOVE

behold, thou art fair; thou hast
doves' eyes.

BRIDE behold, thou art fair, my beloved,
yea, pleasant:
also our bed is green.
the beams of our house are cedar,
and our rafters of fir.

BRIDE i am the rose of sharon,
and the lily of the valleys.

BRIDEGROOM as the lily among thorns,
so is my love among the daughters.

BRIDE as the apple tree among the trees
of the wood,
so is my beloved among the sons.
i sat down under his shadow
with great delight,
and his fruit was sweet to my taste.
he brought me to the banqueting
house,
and his banner over me was love.
stay me with flagons, comfort me
with apples:
for i am sick of love.
his left hand is under my head,
and his right hand doth embrace me.
i charge you, o ye daughters
of jerusalem,

RISE UP, MY LOVE, MY FAIR ONE, AND COME AWAY

By the roes, and by the hinds of the
field, that ye stir not up, nor awake
my love, till he please.
The voice of my beloved! Behold, he
cometh leaping upon the mountains,
skipping upon the hills.
My beloved is like a roe or a young
hart:
Behold, he standeth behind our wall,
he looketh forth at the windows,
shewing himself through the lattice.
My beloved spake, and said unto me,
"Rise up, my love, my fair one,
and come away.
For, lo, the winter is past,
the rain is over and gone;
The flowers appear on the earth;
the time of the singing of birds
is come, and the voice of the turtle
is heard in our land;
The fig tree putteth forth her green
figs, and the vines with the tender
grape give a good smell.
Arise, my love, my fair one,
and come away.
O my dove, that art in the clefts of
the rock, in the secret places
of the stairs,
Let me see thy countenance,

Let me hear thy voice;
for sweet is thy voice, and thy
countenance is comely."
"Take us the foxes,
the little foxes, that spoil the vines:
for our vines have tender grapes."
My beloved is mine, and I am his:
he feedeth among the lilies.
Until the day break, and the
shadows flee away,
Turn, my beloved, and be thou like a
roe or a young hart upon the
mountains of Bether·

BRIDE By night on my bed I sought him
whom my soul loveth:
I sought him, but I found him not·
I will rise now, and go about the city
in the streets, and in the broad ways
I will seek him whom my soul
loveth:
I sought him, but I found him not·
The watchmen that go about the city
found me: to whom I said,
"Saw ye him whom my soul loveth?"
It was but a little that I passed
from them,
But I found him whom my soul loveth:

I held him, and would not let him go,
until I had brought him into my
mother's house,
and into the chamber of her
that conceived me.
I charge you, o ye daughters of
Jerusalem,
by the roes, and by the hinds of the
field,
that ye stir not up, nor awake my love,
till he please.

chorus Who is this that cometh out of the
wilderness like pillars of smoke,
perfumed with myrrh and
frankincense, with all powders of
the merchant?
Behold his bed, which is Solomon's;
threescore valiant men are about it,
of the valiant of Israel.
They all hold swords, being expert
in war:
every man hath his sword upon his
thigh because of fear in the night.
King Solomon made himself a
chariot of the wood of Lebanon.
He made the pillars thereof of silver,
the bottom thereof of gold,
the covering of it of purple,
the midst thereof being paved with

GO FORTH, O YE DAUGHTERS OF ZION,
AND BEHOLD KING SOLOMON

Love, for the daughters of Jerusalem.
Go forth, o ye daughters of Zion, and
behold King Solomon with the crown
wherewith his mother crowned him
in the day of his espousals,
and in the day of the gladness
of his heart.

BRIDEGROOM Behold, thou art fair, my love;
behold, thou art fair;
thou hast doves' eyes within thy locks:
thy hair is as a flock of goats,
that appear from mount Gilead.
thy teeth are like a flock of sheep
that are even shorn, which came up
from the washing;
whereof everyone bear twins, and
none is barren among them.
thy lips are like a thread of scarlet,
and thy speech is comely:
thy temples are like a piece of a
pomegranate within thy locks.
thy neck is like the tower of David
builded for an armoury,
whereon there hang a thousand
bucklers, all shields of mighty men.
thy two breasts are like two young
roes that are twins,

which feed among the lilies.
until the day break, and the shadows
flee away,
i will get me to the mountain of
myrrh, and to the hill of frankincense.
thou art all fair, my love; there is no
spot in thee.
come with me from lebanon,
my spouse, with me from lebanon:
look from the top of amana, from
the top of shenir and hermon, from
the lions' dens, from the mountains
of the leopards.
thou hast ravished my heart,
my sister, my spouse;
thou hast ravished my heart
with one of thine eyes,
with one chain of thy neck.
how fair is thy love, my sister,
my spouse!
how much better is thy love than wine!
and the smell of thine ointments
than all spices!
thy lips, o my spouse, drop as the
honeycomb:
honey and milk are under thy tongue;
and the smell of thy garments is like
the smell of lebanon.
a garden inclosed is my sister,

my spouse; a spring shut up,
a fountain sealed.
thy plants are an orchard of
pomegranates, with pleasant fruits;
camphire, with spikenard,
spikenard and saffron;
calamus and cinnamon, with all
trees of frankincense; myrrh and
aloes, with all the chief spices:
a fountain of gardens, a well of
living waters, and streams from
Lebanon.

BRIDE awake, o north wind; and come, thou
south;
blow upon my garden, that the spices
thereof may flow out.
Let my beloved come into his garden,
and eat his pleasant fruits.

BRIDEGROOM I am come into my garden,
my sister, my spouse:
I have gathered my myrrh with my
spice; I have eaten my honeycomb
with my honey;
I have drunk my wine with my milk:
CHORUS eat, o friends; drink, yea, drink
abundantly, o beloved.
BRIDE I sleep, but my heart waketh:

a garden inclosed is my sister, my spouse

it is the voice of my beloved that
knocketh, saying,
"open to me, my sister, my love,
my dove, my undefiled:
for my head is filled with dew, and
my locks with the drops of night."
"i have put off my coat; how shall
i put it on?
i have washed my feet; how shall i
defile them?"
my beloved put in his hand by the
hole of the door,
and my bowels were moved for him.
i rose up to open to my beloved;
and my hands dropped with myrrh,
and my fingers with sweet smelling
myrrh,
upon the handles of the lock.
i opened to my beloved;
but my beloved had withdrawn
himself, and was gone:
my soul failed when he spake:
i sought him, but i could not find him;
i called him, but he gave me no answer.
the watchmen that went about the
city found me,
they smote me, they wounded me;
the keepers of the walls took away
my veil from me.

I ROSE UP TO OPEN TO MY BELOVED

I charge you, o daughters of
Jerusalem,
if ye find my beloved, that ye tell him,
that I am sick of love.

chorus what is thy beloved more than
another beloved, o thou fairest
among women?
what is thy beloved more than
another beloved, that thou dost so
charge us?

bride my beloved is white and ruddy,
the chiefest among ten thousand.
his head is as the most fine gold,
his locks are bushy, and black as a
raven.
his eyes are as the eyes of doves
by the rivers of waters,
washed with milk, and fitly set.
his cheeks are as a bed of spices,
as sweet flowers:
his lips like lilies, dropping sweet
smelling myrrh.
his hands are as gold rings set with
the beryl:
his belly is as bright ivory overlaid
with sapphires.
his legs are as pillars of marble,
set upon sockets of fine gold:
his countenance is as Lebanon,

excellent as the cedars.
his mouth is most sweet: yea, he is
altogether lovely.
this is my beloved, and this is my friend,
o daughters of jerusalem.

chorus whither is thy beloved gone,
o thou fairest among women?
whither is thy beloved turned aside?
that we may seek him with thee.

bride my beloved is gone down into his
garden, to the beds of spices,
to feed in the gardens, and to gather
lilies.
i am my beloved's, and my beloved
is mine: he feedeth among the lilies.

bridegroom thou art beautiful, o my love, as tirzah,
comely as jerusalem,
terrible as an army with banners.
turn away thine eyes from me, for
they have overcome me:
thy hair is as a flock of goats that
appear from gilead.
thy teeth are as a flock of sheep which
go up from the washing,
whereof every one beareth twins, and
there is not one barren among them.
as a piece of a pomegranate

are thy temples within thy locks.
there are threescore queens, and
fourscore concubines,
and virgins without number.
my dove, my undefiled is but one;
she is the only one of her mother,
she is the choice one of her that
bare her.
the daughters saw her,
and blessed her;
yea, the queens and the concubines,
and they praised her.
who is she that looketh forth as the
morning,
fair as the moon, clear as the sun,
and terrible as an army
with banners?
i went down into the garden of nuts
to see the fruits of the valley, and to
see whether the vine flourished,
and the pomegranates budded.
or ever i was aware,
my soul made me like the chariots
of ammi-nadib.
"return, return, o shulamite;
return, return, that we may look
upon thee."
"what will ye see in the shulamite?
as it were the company of two armies."

she is the choice one of her that bare her

20

BRIDEGROOM how beautiful are thy feet
with shoes, o prince's daughter!
the joints of thy thighs are like jewels,
the work of the hands of a cunning
workman.
thy navel is like a round goblet,
which wanteth not liquor:
thy belly is like an heap of wheat set
about with lilies.
thy two breasts are like two young
roes that are twins.
thy neck is as a tower of ivory;
thine eyes like the fishpools
in heshbon, by the gate of bathrabbim:
thy nose is as the tower of lebanon
which looketh toward damascus.
thine head upon thee is like carmel,
and the hair of thine head like purple;
the king is held in the galleries.
how fair and how pleasant art thou,
o love, for delights!
this thy stature is like to a palm tree,
and thy breasts to clusters of grapes.
i said, "i will go up to the palm tree,
i will take hold of the boughs thereof":
now also thy breasts shall be as
clusters of the vine,

come, my beloved, let us go forth into the field

and the smell of thy nose like apples;
and the roof of thy mouth
like the best wine for my beloved,
that goeth down sweetly,
causing the lips of those that are
asleep to speak.

BRIDE I am my beloved's,
and his desire is toward me.
come, my beloved, let us go forth
into the field;
let us lodge in the villages.
let us get up early to the vineyards;
let us see if the vine flourish,
whether the tender grape appear,
and the pomegranates bud forth:
there will I give thee my loves.
the mandrakes give a smell,
and at our gates are all manner
of pleasant fruits,
new and old,
which I have laid up for thee,
o my beloved.

BRIDE o that thou wert as my brother,
that sucked the breasts
of my mother!
when I should find thee without,
I would kiss thee;

yea, i should not be despised.
i would lead thee, and bring thee into
my mother's house, who would
instruct me:
i would cause thee to drink of spiced
wine of the juice of my pomegranate.
his left hand should be under my head,
and his right hand should embrace me.
i charge you, o daughters of
jerusalem,
that ye stir not up, nor awake my
love, until he please.

CHORUS who is this that cometh up from the
wilderness,
leaning upon her beloved?

BRIDEGROOM i raised thee up under the apple tree:
there thy mother brought thee forth:
there she brought thee forth
that bare thee.

BRIDE set me as a seal upon thine heart,
as a seal upon thine arm:
for love is strong as death;
jealousy is cruel as the grave:
the coals thereof are coals of fire,
which hath a most vehement flame.
many waters cannot quench love,
neither can the floods drown it:
if a man would give all the
substance of his house for love,

24

it would utterly be contemned.
chorus "we have a little sister,
and she hath no breasts:
what shall we do for our sister
in the day when she shall
be spoken for?
if she be a wall, we will build upon
her a palace of silver:
and if she be a door, we will inclose
her with boards of cedar."
bride i am a wall, and my breasts
like towers:
then was i in his eyes as one that
found favour.
solomon had a vineyard at
baal-hamon;
he let out the vineyard unto keepers;
every one for the fruit thereof
was to bring a thousand pieces
of silver.
my vineyard, which is mine,
is before me:
thou, o solomon, must have a
thousand,
and those that keep the fruit thereof
two hundred.
bridegroom thou that dwellest in the gardens,
the companions hearken to thy voice:
cause me to hear it.

I RAISED THEE UP UNDER THE APPLE TREE

BRIDE make haste, my beloved,
and be thou like to a roe or to a
young hart
upon the mountains of spices.

This book was designed by Larry Brady. The introduction was set in Garth Graphic on a Compugraphic 8600 Digital Typesetter. The text was calligraphed by Marsha Brady in a modernized Uncial style developed by Larry Brady. Color Separations are by Color Graphics, San Diego, California. The binding is by Automated Bindery, Los Angeles, California.

Printed by The Green Tiger Press